NIGHT OPEN

NIGHT OPEN
Selected Poems of Rolf Jacobsen

TRANSLATED BY OLAV GRINDE

WHITE PINE PRESS · FREDONIA, NEW YORK

Translation, Introduction and Interview
Copyright © 1993 by Olav Grinde

An earlier version of the introductory essay
was first published in *Northern Light*

The interview appeared previously in *South Dakota Review.*

Some of the translations have previously appeared in *The Christian
Science Monitor, Whole Earth Review, Translation, Scandinavian Review,
California Quarterly, Webster Review, The Montana Review, Stone Country,
Mr.Cognito, Pulp, Paintbrush, Permafrost, South Dakota Review, Stand,
Chapman, Northern Light,*and *Pacific Quarterly/Moana.* Several were also
included in the anthologies *Twenty Contemporary Norwegian Poets*
(Norway) and *Modern Poetry in Translation: 1983* (England).

The translator wishes to thank Rolf Jacobsen, Lloyd Baskerville,
Dennis Maloney, Øyvind Haaland, and Michael Anderson
for comments and suggestions.

Publication of this book was made possible, in part, by grants from
the National Endowment for the Arts,the New York State
Council on the Arts, and Norwegian Literature Abroad.

Printed in the United States of America

First Edition

Book design by Watershed Design
Cover photograph of Northern Lights by Trym Ivar Bergsmo
Author photograph by Tom A. Kolstad

ISBN 0-877727-33-4

9 8 7 6 5 4 3 2 1

WHITE PINE PRESS
10 Village Square
Fredonia, New York 14063

CONTENTS

NIGHT OPEN (1985)

NIGHT OPEN

INTRODUCTION

SEEDS OF FIRE

Rolf Jacobsen is a poet of silence and light. He sees the tiny snail in the grass "who wanders on a kiss" and "old people's graves . . . very quiet and with sunbleached stones." He speaks gently of the blind man "who knows what dreams are made of" and "can tell from your voice if you heart is at peace."

But upon reading the poetry of Rolf Jacobsen it soon becomes apparent that he lives in the twentieth century. With a penetrating vision he writes of the city and machines as perhaps no one else. He notices the antennae "sparse as a forest of crosses / on the city's roofs," and asks, "who sleeps here / in these deep graves?"

Rolf Jacobsen is not a newcomer to poetry; his literary career spans half a century. Jacobsen was born in Oslo, the capital of Norway, in 1907. When he was six, he moved to the countryside, "where I went through a second birth." He has lived for many years in Hamar, northeast of Oslo, where he worked as a journalist for a local newspaper. His first book, *Earth and Iron,* came out in 1933. United in the title are references to the world of nature and the hard-edged world created by twentieth-century man, which Jacobsen will deal with again and again in his poetry. Here are poems such as "Rain," "Saltwater," "Clouds," but also "Harbor," "Power Line," and "Industrial District." And the city's "sound is the echo of your own clattering footsteps." With due reason, Jacobsen is given much of the credit for introducing modern poetry into Norwegian literature.

Immediately we become aware of a great honesty and freedom that manifests itself in clarity. We are not struck by a great show of technique but rather a self-acceptance that takes the form of a sudden relaxation of language. In this way, he frees himself from the influence of nineteenth-century English poetry and writes twentieth-century poems that are clearly Norwegian. As Robert Bly has said, his lines are no longer "soldiers standing at attention."

He builds his poem around the image, with music that is closer to the sound of the wind blowing through the pines, of the North Sea washing over the skerries in calm weather than to the sound of the metronome. He does experiment with rhyme and with the iambic and other rhythmic patterns — and does so successfully — but always he returns to a natural style of poetry that he makes his own.

The Norwegian language seems ideally suited for Jacobsen's poetry. Like English, it is a Germanic language, but its greater musicality stems from Old Norse. The language, now in a very dynamic state of change, lies somewhere between the lyrical language of the Swede (much imitated and parodied in Hollywood movies), and that of the Dane (who is constantly accused of swallowing his consonants). There is a sense of great age in the Norwegian language; intricately interwoven with it is the psychic history of a people; its sounds seem to flow directly from the landscape. In one poem, Jacobsen gives homage to the old Norwegian place names. It's as though they were "hacked out of the mountains." But he admits:

> *There must have lived someone here before us*
> *who knew the place in a way we've lost.*

Most Americans have heard of the "midnight sun" — when the sun never sets. In "Northern Lights," Jacobsen writes compellingly of the Norwegian winter, when the sun in vain tries to lift its feeble torch above the horizon. His heightened treatment of this moment touches on the timeless experience engraved in Norwegian consciousness. The Norwegian landscape, psychic as well as geographic, shows up in Jacobsen's poems. But he is not a narrow literary nationalist like Henrik Wergeland; his poem "Church on Wall Street," for example, goes beyond national concerns as well as national borders; and English words (which continually enter the Norwegian language via music, films, advertisements, tourism, and the petroleum industry) show up in his poems without prejudice.

Earth and Iron is a slim collection of thirty-three poems. His second book, *Swarm,* published two years later, contains thirty-two. Then Jacobsen becomes silent for many years until, in 1951, he inaugurates a new creative period with *Express Train* — again a slim volume of thirty poems. His new books, arriving every three or four years, carry titles such as *Secret Life* (1954), *Summer in the Grass* (1956), *Letter to Light* (1960), *The Silence Afterwards* (1965), *Headlines* (1969), *Watch the Doors — the Doors Are Closing* (1972), *Breathing Exercise* (1975), *Think About Something Else* (1979), and, in 1985, *Night Open*.

His poems take form slowly by American standards, as evidenced by his small output and by the sometimes remarkable difference between an early version published in the daily press and the finished product.

Creation often takes time, both God's and man's. In "Coral" he describes how layer grows upon layer until "thundering light bursts forth." And what happens? "Soil comes, rain comes / sprouting seeds come..."

And the seeds do come. Rolf Jacobsen may well be described as a sower of inner seeds of fire. His poems are pregnant with meaning that stretches far beyond words.

He asks in a straightforward fashion:

What sower has walked over the Earth,
what hands have sown
our inner seeds of fire?

Jacobsen plants his seeds without any violence. He does not use big knives to tear open the earth of the reader's mind. No. He writes for those who are still "half-awake," as he puts it; for those who still have some curiosity left; for those who are able to pick up a book before they turn out the lights. But months, even years later, many have experienced how a phrase or an image returns and speaks to them, almost in the gentle whisper of their guardian angel.

The poet knows how hard it is for us to let reality in. Not the media-reality that overwhelms and numbs, but Truth. In a poem in *Night Open*, he compares Truth to a sick girl with a child in her arms, who waits outside your door:

> *What do you do? If you open*
> *it will change your life.*
>
> *Do you hesitate?*
> *You, too.*

Jacobsen is not an intensely personal poet like Olaf Bull; he is very much concerned with the outer world as well. In a powerful and precise statement of our condition in this age, he says:

> *— whatever we do*
> *the machines*
> *only move the hunger two stairs up;*
> *now it sits in the heart.*

In his letter "To Earth," he speaks about man's loss of inner balance. The result is a "landscape with steam shovels" and "skyhigh houses" where man's condition is "to grow downward." He voices his concern over the planet's survival. But his views are not those of Robinson Jeffers; he does see hope — if only we change the direction of our path. But, as he says:

> *In East and West the slums grow like a disease*
> *and have already formed a crust around*
> *the large cities.*

19

And he speaks of the sidewalks

*. . . that one day shall be present at the
world's end
and cry out to the heavens and the ocean:*

Here we have 'em.

His later poems grow more and more power-
ful; one may feel a need to put his last books aside
for days after reading a single poem. At eighty-six,
Rolf Jacobsen sees very clearly what is happening in
the world. These are the poems of a man who is
looking down the barrel of the gun. His poem "Roses
— Roses" freezes to an image preceding the crucifix-
ion. He says of our long-repressed shadow-side,
which in distorted form is again rising to the surface
in the Western psyche:

You have it in you.
Far inside you someplace.
The yellow, staring eye. And the thought
that is colder than ice.

and

What are we doing?
Giving it over to the night?
Well hidden.
Yes.
No.

He remembers the Nazi "road projects" of

World War II. In "Asphalt" he writes of the frightening prospect of the control of traffic in our minds. He writes of the waterfall which gives its life for the sake of lighted advertising in the cities — advertising that screams at us, and finally shouts to those who see past, are not attracted to this light, and continue walking: "Stop. Or we shoot."

Titles such as "Big City," "The Church on Wall Street," and "Bethlehem Steel" say much about the poem. Yet with tenderness he writes:

The man with the white cane has enough
time.
If he takes your hand he feels its bones
like birdwings.

And in a beautiful poem about the "Black Man," in the last verse, he says:

Our new brother
who had the Earth's face
and got to suckle the Earth's breast longest.
Maybe it will be he — in the end,
who inherits it all.

In 1985, he published *Night Open,* which sold a record 18,500 copies. Given that there are little more than four million people in Norway, that would be comparable to a new volume of poetry selling more than a million copies in the United States.

In March 1992, scholars, critics, translators, teachers and lovers of his poetry gathered for a two-day seminar on Rolf Jacobsen's work at Flisa, the town where he grew up. It is the first time such an honor has been bestowed upon a living Norwegian poet.

Rolf Jacobsen has consistently kept the private and personal out of his poetry. The notable exception is the grief-work expressed in the love poems to Petra, his wife of forty-three years, in *Night Open*. He once said: "You know, we only argued once during all those years. That ended when she threw a boot at me and we both burst out laughing." Such relationships are rare.

He stands beside her grave and feels little desire to continue alone:

Friend beyond death. Take me down to you.
— Under the snow. Under the brown wreath.

Henrik Ibsen has said that being a poet means being able to see. Jacobsen sees the secret connections between things. There is a sense of great depth in the interweaving of associations in his poems. Much like a first-rate composer, he incorporates silence into his work, lending a wonderful feeling of space to his poems. Often the "not-words" seem much more important than what is actually said with words. After reading such a poem its silence opens up within us, and things and experiences that had been forgotten begin to move within that space. In this respect he resembles the Swedish poet Tomas Tranströmer, familiar to many American readers.

Rolf Jacobsen sees the unseeable, but also small details and aspects of our existence that usually pass unnoticed. Jacobsen, a Catholic, does not separate the spiritual from the worldly. It penetrates and breathes through the world seen with his eyes. How beautifully he writes about the old:

> *The lines on old people's hands*
> *gradually curve over and will soon point*
> *toward earth.*

Bly points out that he sees the old as spiritual beings — slowly they become transparent as the edges of their human egos fade:

> *The old*
> *who gradually become themselves once more*
> *and slowly dissolve*
> *like smoke, unnoticed they pass over*
> *into sleep*
> *and light.*

Jacobsen writes poetry as though he is painting. His best poems have a wonderful translucence; he creates windows that give you a very clear view of what he sees. Suddenly he changes scale, and the poem expands in a burst of light. The Earth, he says, is a blossom

> *on the star tree*
> *pale and with luminous ocean leaves.*

In "Breathing Exercise" he takes you out until you see the entire universe

only as a flash, just as
lonely, as distant
as a star on a June night

and tells you:

and still, my friend, if you go
far enough out
you are only at the beginning

— of yourself.

— Olav Grinde
Bergen, Norway
August 1993

EARTH AND IRON

(1933)

A MATTED WINDOWPANE

Toward all the walls of painted concrete,
and toward the snow of paper,
and through thunder from typewriters in the room,
shines this pane of matted glass
into a bright, bright office.

No sun is brighter
and no day is bluer than the one
we sense out there
beyond the pane's white shadowplay.

The papers snow and snow,
a distant sink groans.
Above bent backs
through that pale window
we sense the flight of clouds.

SALTWATER

1.

The ocean forms large houses and tears them down
        again.
The heart that can't find any peace must forever
        search,
rummaging with enormous hands through clouds
        and chasms.

Can you hear the deep voice sing and shout out
        there?
Or cry silently, breathe violently at night.
Searches but can't find its way,
rushes against all lands on Earth
and is thrown back with a sigh.

Or the star night.
When the world's cool sweat bursts forth and glitters
and drips as snow towards the deep,
sails around as melting flakes out there, sways
        and tips
in the slow blue hours before the sun arrives
from other oceans.

— The sun's white eye.
The fever eye, white with a bloody pupil
that can't blink and never
closes.

The ocean forms large houses and tears them down
        again.

The heart that can't find any peace must search
        forever.
The tidewater's sweeping breath
lifts the transparent mountains toward the moon
and lays them down again, quietly.
The heavy snake-colored body lies breathing,
tied in a ring around the Earth. It shakes in spasms
and slaps its white fin against rocky shores,
rages over all the skerries
so the land shakes and vibrates
far up in grey mountain pastures,
far inside green forests.

2.

Then an arm of night-dark
marble is thrown against the land's heart.
The fjord's pale sun-veins
seek the glacier's breasts.

The large fjord wanders ghostlike
toward headland after headland in shadow
and winds its turbulent seafloor
around collapsing mountains,

turns toward new coves,
opens large gates inward
toward Ringøyno, Månsnes, Tytlandsvik cove
with those white pebble beaches

into the large grotto
where light dives in from high cathedral windows,

sun-red, brass yellow, lead-bordered
onto the slate-stone floor of the fjord.

The glaciers ride in the light, distant
on gold horses. Rivers fall.
The grey tide
shatters the clinging glass fingers.
Foam spray
in deep shadow.

3.

By the low Fishrock
you can see against the skyline
in good weather
stones lie strewn in the water
while the ocean plays, white and blue
and sprays the brown shore
with flashing sunlight.

There it lies in the sun and storm
a land in grey, in green and white
with crag and kelp, tideline
and fishcove

and heavily lifts its bellclang
from headland to headland for a thousand miles
along the coast as far as it goes
— a wreath of foam, a wreath of song
and gull cries.

POWER LINE

Beneath plummeting mountain walls rises
        a resounding dark song.
The low church down there with its marble vaults
lifts its hymn with all its might and binds the wild
        demons,
opens its sad embrace for the repentant heart.

Tempered in steel fonts and baptized by these husky
        turbines
the army of redemption rises jubilantly toward
        hillside and forest,
advances through the hills in snow-white lace coats
and lifts its shining wings of steel in trembling
        expectancy.

Away through forests, onward day and night
the shining armies roam with the living word
        for the world.

Meet them at night by the dark mountain farm
        and hear
how they speak in tongues and struggle
        with the night and the Lord.

Lightning cuts the air, the humming of dazzling
        wings,
roads meet, valley and sun radiantly.
Down from the mountain with song and trembling
        hands they carry
holy fire from heaven to the land.

SOUNDS

It isn't
tires smacking rainwet asphalt
that is the city's sound.

It isn't
the milktruck's squeak against sidewalks
on grey mornings. The rushing metro.

It isn't
the silent flicker of neon signs
above living rivers,
nor the arc lamps' glittering
pearlbands.

Not the clinking of glasses
in large noisy restaurants.
The steamboat's raw howl in the harbor:
two short, one long — two short, one long.

It isn't
the deafening song of the streetcar at night
against streets you don't know.
The saxophone from the fifth floor.

No.
The city's sound,
the city's racing pulse
you will notice one night
(the night you walk lonely and without hope
for the first time)
rising as a resounding scorn
from the stone street behind you:
— Your own clattering footsteps.

FLYING MACHINES

Aluminum:
> Summer Sunday.
> Leaves lit by sun.
> Snow.

Aluminum:
> Fish scales.
> Oil-grey swells above the ocean's gathering
> > wrath.

> Pantherskin
> stretched over muscles tensed for the leap.

Aluminum:
> Fields tremble.
> Wings darken against the sky.
> Engines drill screaming into the sun.

TRAVEL

The station waiting room at night
with that chilly air of raw cement
and iron,
with rows of dried up sandwiches
under glass,
stacked chairs in the shadows,
streams running over platforms from the cleaning
        women's mops
in the damp morning hours
can fill my soul with fierceness.

Travel toward foreign countries.
Smoke through compartment windows, the rails'
magical songs. — Paris, Marseille.

When the asphalt has worn my feet
to embers,
when the shop windows' glittering eyes
have lost their spell
and my world stands still and only
stares at me,
I often go to the train stations
where the white smoke columns draw happy
question marks on the sky,
or to the harbor
where large ships lie fragrant with
paint and ocean, their hulls luminous.

I want to ride on the prow of such a ship
toward a new city.

I want to hear the waves play around the hull
as we slowly glide in toward
hazy towers and old bridges through smoke.

And I want to hear the street noise rise,
the streetcars toll strange new sounds.

I want to feel the smell of chestnut buds
drift toward the harbor. Chestnut buds and exhaust.

HARBOR

All streets and markets end here.
Dust brown cobblestone miles
widen and stop.

Light dives into the city.
Harbor.

After the hungry days
the docks' good noise, the clamor of plate-iron.
I arrive at the silo-cube
and the hundred grey warehouses.
— Now I see my garden grow toward the sky,
the forest of towering steam-trees:
blue-black, reddish brown
with dazzling white flowers.

S.S. Brunla will sail tonight.
Wicker chairs shine on deck, fragrant with fresh
        lacquer.
Suitcases are stowed. Winches bark vehemently.
Beneath the steaming, tilting hulls
traincars glide quietly with fish and lumber.

The ocean has iron palisades.
The propellors growl
behind grey, black and red iron
fortresses against the land of cobblestones.

Ghost-shadows
glide over the sea-milk beyond.
— Blenda of Hamburg.
Masts advance on the sky.
Laughingly the crane swings
a yellow banner in the morning grey sky.
A hundred crates in the air.
Oranges.
— San Pedro de Toros, Valencia!

AFTERNOON

The car stops at the corner.
The street lies silent and white.
The curtains' lazy banners sway
over a world of shadow and dust.

All the dining rooms are deserted now.
Silver vases gleam on red
mahogany buffets in half-darkness.
On heavy, feebly-glowing buffets in shadow
stand copper trays of fruit.

It is now all the strange patterns awaken.
The peacock on the silk screen. The embroidered
        fields of flowers.
Dust sylphs play
in forests of oak leaves. And from the Chinese
        temple
flows a low music.

All the dining rooms are deserted now.
Citizen, it is the hour when you rest.
Only that large buffet is alive
and the silk screen and the flower vase.
While the carpet dust
dances in the ray from
newlit streetlights.

The ships howl in the harbor.
The sidewalks outside are wet.

METAPHYSICS OF THE CITY

Beneath gutter gratings,
beneath moldy brick cellars,
beneath the boulevards' moist linden roots
and park lawns:

The nerve-network of telephone cables
The gas pipes' hollow arteries.
Sewers.

From the east side's human alps,
to the west side villas hidden behind spirea
—the same unseen links of iron and copper
bind us together.

No one can hear the telephone cables' crackling life.
No one can hear the gas pipes' diseased cough
        from the abyss.
No one can hear the sewers roar with slime
        and stench for a hundred miles in darkness.
The city's ironclad entrails
are at work.

But up in the daylight you dance with lively
feet over the asphalt, with silk against your navel's
        white eye, and a new coat in the sunlight

And somewhere in the daylight I stand and watch
the cigarette's blue soul flutter like a chaste angel
through the chestnut leaves on its way toward
        eternal life.

SWARM

(1935)

TIRES

A pale morning in June at 4 A.M.
when the country roads are still grey and moist
through endless tunnels of forests,
a car has driven over the dirt road
where the ant is out, busy with his pine needle now,
wandering in the huge G of "Goodyear"
pressed into the sandy road
for a hundred and twenty kilometers.
Pine needles are heavy.
Again and again he slides back down
        with his unbalanced load
and works his way up again
and slips back again.
Travelling across the great Sahara lit by clouds.

NORTHERN LIGHTS

The day that ascends with tears in its throat
behind ragged horizons is not
a real day, but
all the dead
disowned days which never found a heart.
Misery's day, hunger's and the frost's, that
sneak here at night and try
to shine some sun and pour a little light
from hungering, wizened breasts.

Timidly it lifts
its face now, behind a hundred forests
and stares with burning eyes
out over lands it is not allowed to love.

Now it moves its fingers
and shakes the black bars of night
and tries again and again to light its smoldering
          sun,
but it withers,
dwindles and is snuffed out by the cold.
Far to the west — in the outermost east
it tries to slip through, but the night's
walls are built of granite
and its columns of steel.

Stare out the windows,
come bareheaded out on the roads, and stand
in clusters by the crossroads:
Slowly the struggler's arms sink.
Mutely she rends her clothes,

then burns them
on the cold's radiant fire.
Smoke
flares up over the woods
Smoke
thrusts down above the fir-tops and the low houses
        on the heath.
Smoke
freezes to ice on the sky, so morning
arrives with streaks of weeping.

REALITY

The day we cling to:
Shops where we buy fancy clothes. Trips
we'll soon take.
The streets' tumult. The rain on sidewalks
at dusk
    is dream.
        Night and insomnia.
        Worries about money.
        Good fortune that never comes is reality.

The security in large roaring crowds.
Speed.
Blaring bands and thrilling thick newspapers
    is dream and shadow.
        Eyes of the praying man.
        The hands of the freezing one.
        The trudging of all those who wander
        hungry through large cities
        is reality.

Long interesting debates. Arguments
(from one side and the other side).
The lecterns, the priests, the fanfare of trumpets.
The drums, the rhythm, the rush that drives us on
    is dream.
        The machine guns.
        Bloody fields and mud. Your cry
        when you one night awake to the suffering.
        The snow on the field hospitals.
        The mass graves, are reality.

The sod that keeps growing.
Grasses bending softly in the wind.
The song of waves
is reality.

COBBLESTONE

Stomp us down in the dust, bolt us down and forget,
but our muscles carry the world
and feel their strength grow beneath the load.

Paper, banana peels, black gutters
and neon signs, dazzling shops.
Look, our armies reach to the ends of the Earth.

New York and London we carry in silence.
We're silent beneath the limousine
and hold our composure until our knuckles turn
        white.

Children of granite. Hardened in the volcano forge.
Carved from the Earth's bones to carry burdens.
Nineveh, Rome — we were there.

We were in place in blue Atlantis.
We saw the new continents
brush off waves and rise toward light.

And one day when we feel the Earth tremble
below heavy shoes on their way toward a new age
— O grey brothers above, let us follow.

MOSS, RUST AND MOTHS

Moss comes out of the earth.
Silent as the bats of night
it settles on stones and waits,
or down in the grass
with ashen wings.

Rust goes from bolt to bolt,
from iron plate to iron plate in darkness,
and carefully examines
if the time is right.
When pistons have gone to rest,
when the support columns have arrived in the heart
        of night,
then it shall do its silent, bloody work.

The star-moths
sit in clusters on the dark windows of heaven
and stare
and stare at the city lights.

GRAIN

Now all the tiny grains rest in the earth
with hand under cheek and mutter and crackle
      in the darkness
and dream they fall dizzily down through
dark chasms,
and now it is only life that nudges them
to hasten and grow.
One morning a nose apears between the lumps
      of earth
and soon a whole shoulder.
They stretch out their arms in the light
      and straighten their backs
and touch each other's eyes
— shoulder to shoulder over half a world.

The animal-shaped clouds lift their heads
up over the horizon
and seem as unfathomable as sphinxes
with snow-white foreheads and hectic stains on their
      cheeks.
They rise and glide into space
without a sound.

The wind comes one evening to feel if the tittering
ears won't be ripe soon.
It goes around and lifts slender arms
and feels green knees with brisk
fingers.
And all gasp at the touch and realize
at once they are naked and cold.
They feel the good shame

rush up to their ears and out into the wispy fingers.
Soon the fields stand white as fire and
hum over half the world.

The Earth wraps itself in its blue oceans at night
and cleanses itself with
dew early every morning, looks at its breasts
and feels them grow and turn hard
as ivory under sun and clouds.

— Soon the flour flows white as milk through
the mill's greedy teeth.
In the breaden jars we carry it out
to the hungry.
For the Earth has opened its green robe
to let its little ones
drink again.

CRUST ON FRESH SNOW

My soul is hard as stone. I slept with the wind.
He's an unfaithful lover. Now he's with someone else.
He hummed words, prattled in my ear
and stroked my hair. I gave him all my whiteness.
I let him chisel dreams in my soul — of clouds,
fierce seas, and soft flowery hills.
Now I see, cold, it was them he loved.
Where is he now? Tonight my heart froze.

TREMBLING TELEPHONE POLES

The sound of the stars' heavy millstones
that slowly grind around huge hubs, and
turn their frozen faces toward each other
and turn away again behind a billion miles,
— all things that move through space
on gigantic ball bearings send out low sounds,
whining songs that die across the vast distances.
This is what we hear in the hum from telephone
        wires;
they're antennae that catch signals from space
and shout them out on empty hillsides at night
when telephone poles stand murmuring
        and anxiously call out,
as when a person dreams dark dreams
and something pinches his heart, painful thoughts
he doesn't understand, that press their way through
        his throat
but die in the mouth and become only broken cries
— that's the sound of all stars.
It always howls like that out in space.

SWARM

In story above story, on street after street, they bend over their machines, hunch over desks or work counters and bars, let their hands move, but never reveal with a face nor twitch of an eye that they often sit alone, hunched over numbers on small scraps of paper, sums, dates, and walk around with numbers in their hearts, numbers that gnaw their limbs like trichonosis and keep them awake at night: How can I make it. What will happen to us.

We meet on the streetcar or on the escalator; our eyes meet for a second, then never again. The sidewalks are full of people who rush past each other in endless crowds, but not one confesses to another that he walks around with an arithmetic problem in his heart, and that his feet are chained with clattering numbers, hard as steel, sharp as thorns. What will happen when they find out: This is how it is with me.

Those whitewashed houses along roadsides with cheerful picket fences dancing along the windshield or blind curtains you can see from the train for miles — they don't reveal that here lives someone imprisoned by numbers and fear for the days a week from now or two months, a death struggle with numbers and the fear: What will happen to us all.

Where two streets meet we make a park, raise bronze statues of men in long coats and let them stare into space with solemn faces. Newspapers pour into the world their fine clichés of men with firm eyes and clenched lips we refer to with awe, but not one word that they're people like you and me who often sit alone, hunched over numbers on small scraps of paper, sums, dates, struggling with numbers that won't rest at night: How can I make it. What will happen when they find out: This is how it is with me.

EROSION

Gentle brooks draw lines crisscross
like furrows on the land's open hands,
work with invisible files,
saw across a stone knot,
pound a marble corner with their silver hammers
and with quick movements carry it off to the sea.
With their quiet tools
they file off rough flint,
lay it on the shore and start again,
like some silent piano piece.

RED DAWN

Isn't the red dawn our enemy?
With wailing whips it wakes all life,
setting mountains and sea afire.
Tell me why the smoke columns stand blood-red
        in the sunrise
when the day has touched them with its fingers.
It doesn't come to us with roses
but blood.

It touches young girls and makes their hips
and breasts swell,
and their cheeks redden, ignited by blood,
then it is taken away again,
and we are left behind with ashes in our hearts.

Isn't the red dawn our enemy?
See — it comes like a tyrant with whizzing thongs
        in its hands
and hounds us always
onward.

Bloody fingers
grab the world by the throat. Hurry,
onward!

EXPRESS TRAIN

(1951)

COBALT

Colors are the words' little sisters. They could never
        be soldiers.
Secretly I have loved them long.
They shall stay home and hang up sheer curtains
in our everyday bedrooms, kitchen and alcove.

Young Crimson is close to my heart, and brown
        Sienna
but even more thoughtful Cobalt
        with those distant eyes and unbreached mind.

We walk through dew.
The night sky and southern oceans
are her possessions
and that tear-jewel on her forehead:
Cassiopeia's pearls.
We walk through dew late at night.

But the others.
Meet them one morning in June at 4 A.M.
when they rush to meet you
for a morning swim in green coves' spray
Then you can sun yourself with them on the smooth
        rock-face.
— Who would you own?

THE THISTLE'S SUMMER

The thistle's summer has also lain hidden in earth.
In blind seeds it has lain there: a sleeping thought,
    blue crown.

For one day the thistle's summer shall also rise out
    of the earth;
like storks they'll stretch their long necks
along roadsides and in fields, stiffly listening,
    expectant, singing
with life in each fiber and cell. Today, today our
    summer has come,
dreamed deeply in the heart of God.

Open your eyes, thistle — your day has come.
Don't be ashamed of your humble clothes.
The bumblebees wait for you, dragonflies,
    and the joyful frogs along roadsides.
For you have also been given a light to carry, mild
    as the glow in the eyes of animals:
Patience.

LEAVES

I am leaves sprouting only for a time,
a shot of green from a dense trunk of kin.
I stand here a short while and drink joy
until the sun dies in autumn, and it's all over.

But sap rises now from secret depths
and I must sway here with young hopes
and catch the sun for these old giants
who in vain lift me toward heaven.

So large a hope in all things; so dismal a conclusion.
I am a sheen around the Earth. Later nothing.
But I still have sunlight across my forehead
and large forests awake in my heart.

FROSTED WINDOW

Star-swarm!
Look, there's frost on the window. It is the stars
crackling like frozen dew on Earth's window.
Let's breathe on them,
extend our heart's sign,
our young warmth to the sleeping crystals,
so they turn to tears of joy, smilingly
stream away, and allow us
a glimpse of storm-blue sky.

OCEAN

Deep in a bay in the sea of God lie a billion starfires
strewn like fish eggs over banks of night where our
      awareness
first rose from gleaming seeds and now, cold, seeks
lower toward dizzying depths or in shoals toward
      unseen shores,
in those blue depths, toward that sun of suns which
      our eyes
never get to see, but we feel as sparks of gold
      on our forehead.

SUNFLOWER

What sower has walked over the Earth,
what hands have sown
our inner seeds of fire?

Like rainbow curves they went out from his hands
to frozen earth, young loam, hot sand.
There they shall sleep
greedily and drink our life
and blast it to pieces
for the sake of a sunflower you don't know,
or a thistle crown or a chrysanthemum.

Let the young rain of tears come;
let the mild hands of grief come.
It's not as terrible as you think.

EPISTLE

What eternity slants down toward grass
where beetles walk,
what worlds of faith behind the light of a rose.

Pain, so mysterious, how it burns
in swelling buds. Your want,
your love.

Now time slants down toward all fields,
the stars' time, green,
and writes "rose" here and "grass" there
without your help, and the Earth
fills them slowly with its sacrifice
and longing for a wakeful heart.

DAY AND NIGHT

Endless our day —
it is without end.
It only goes away to another place,
moves silently away for a little while,
throws the blue coat around its shoulders,
rinses its feet in the ocean and goes away
then comes running back again with rosy cheeks
and with cool, good hands
lifts your chin and looks you in the face:
— Are you awake yet?

Endless our night—
it is without end.
It only goes away to another place
a little while,
then it's here again
with its feverish eyes
and hair dripping wet as with sweat
and looks at you, and looks at you:
— Why aren't you sleeping?

There is no end to the joy, nor to the pain,
nor to death, nor to life.
They only go away for a little while, they circle
        the Earth
to another heart,
a little while,
then they're back again with their halting voices:
—Are you sleeping? Are you awake?

There is no end to the stars and the wind.
It is only you
who are not the one you think.

SECRET LIFE

(1954)

LANDSCAPE WITH STEAM SHOVELS

They eat of my forests.
Six steam shovels came and ate of my forests.
God help me, what a shape they had. Heads
without eyes and eyes in their rear.

They swing their maws on long shafts,
with dandelions in their mouth-corners.

They eat and spit out, spit out and eat,
because they no longer have a throat, only a huge
mouth and a rumbling gut.
Is this a kind of hell?

For wading birds? For the much-too-wise
pelicans?

They have blinded eyes and chains on their feet.
They shall work centuries and chew the bluebells
into asphalt. Cover them with clouds of thick
        exhaust
and cold sun from the headlights.

Without throats, without vocal chords, without
        complaint.

SHOPS

1.

The glass shop sells invisible things.
They tinkle like spinet music,
and are brittle as the floats of seaweed.

This is the schizoids' house, those who have
ice in their chests and perfect dreams.
The sophisticates, coiled around themselves.

The glass person lives in the kingdom of light,
filled with beauty, but sterile
as the aesthetician.

Letters on glass
are like rain in the eyes.

2.

The hardware store shelves
are the vestries of human thought.
Here they enthrone holy vessels
which form our lives. Casseroles,
both enameled ones and those which show
grey steel.

Here are ideas worked out by the seven wise men
for our sakes. Hammers to pound them in,
tongs to pull them out again,
also sandpaper.

Fireworks on the left and rifles across the street.

3.

The yarn shop is our little cafe
for love affairs. Thus it helps
preserve life.
There can be much compassion
in shiny knitting needles
and deep devotion
in a sweater and green scarf.

Here are secret recipes
and magic runes for your soul.
Good wool smells like young shoots,
sap and heart juice.

4.

But the paint store is closest to my heart.
It shares the secret elixirs of earth,
yellow ochre, turpentine and potter's clay
smelling of decay and birth
— a pharmacy for health in this world.

Once upon a time a paint store owner
married a knitting woman. They grew into
a noble tapestry
and very old. Wove themselves into each other
with light and dark thread into an image of deer
beneath oak, greyed together
in silver and green.

STREET LAMP

My street lamp is so glacially alone in the night.
Small cobblestones cuddle their heads in close
where it holds its light-umbrella over them
so that the wicked darkness will not come near.

It says: We are all far from home.
There's no hope anymore.

MORNING CROWS

The crows wake up the country
with their tired din above the fields,
like rattling steel buckets in the greyish light.
Kra, kra.

And in the cities it is the cleaning women,
kra, kra,
who come clattering with their gear over
        the platforms
and up the stairs and across all the floors
with that tired sound of buckets,
flapping heavily with washcloths and brooms
through morning clouds from soapwater,

while they pick up all the matches
and stick their heads together and gossip
and scurry on home again and sit down to rest
a while
with head under wing.
Kra, kra, kra.

TIMBER

It's good there's still timber
and enough piling sites
in the world.
Because there's a great calm within timber
and a large light in it
that can shine far into the evenings
in summertime.

There's a reassurance in smoke from clearings
and in sap that swells out in large pearls
deep in the forests.
The smell of timber brings to mind sweet poppies
        and grain.

It's good there's still a glow from the timber
        on the heaths
by Ångerman River and Deep Creek, Columbia,
like remnants of sunlight still
embracing the world,
a sleeping strength on earth, a secret force
that will last generations, like iron.

It has the color of bread or a woman's body,
and that shining will that perhaps comes
from great love.

For timber is part of the great Spring in the world.
It grows from sources the ravager hasn't reached
        yet.

*   *   *

The big rivers take care of it.
There's a love between the wood's power
        and the water's.
Rivers move timber slowly around headlands in that
        calm dance-like rhythm.

*   *   *

It's these things the constellations are placed above:
the solitude of the dead, the courage of youth,
        and timber
moving slowly along on large rivers.

MOTHERS

The mothers of this world, they stand like forests
     behind mist.

Half turned away into darkness so no one can see
     their faces.
Nameless and innumerable, a sigh goes out from
     them; they are out in the evenings,
     calling someone through the centuries.

They are the Earth's true citizens. They have
     breasts like full
moons and hips like broad timber.

Stripped of branches and betrayed in the end, they
     pass into darkness
as a memory, a thick wall beam, heavy
as iron.

GUARDIAN ANGEL

I am the bird who taps on your window
       in the morning,
the companion you can never know,
flowers lighting up for the blind.

I am the glacier shining above the forests
and the voices going out from the bell-towers.
The thought that hits you all at once at mid-day
and fills you with such unspeakable joy.

I am the one you loved long ago.
I walk beside you all day and watch you intently.
I lay my mouth against your heart
though you do not know.

I am your third arm and your second
shadow, the white one
you don't have the heart for,
but who can never forget you.

THE OLD WOMEN

The young women with lightning-quick feet,
    where have they gone?
They had knees like small kisses and sleeping hair.

In the far reaches of time, when they've become
    quiet
old ladies with slender hands who slowly climb
    the stairs

with huge keys in their bags, and look around
and talk to little children by the cemetery gates.

In that strange vast land where winters are long
and no one understands their words anymore.

Bow deeply and greet them with respect, for
they still carry it, like a fragrance,

a secret bite in their cheeks, a twitching nerve deep
in the palm of their hands gives them away.

WHEN WE SLEEP

We are all children when we sleep.
There's no war in us then.
We open our hands and breathe
in that calm rhythm heaven has given us.

We all let go of our lips like small children
and open our hands halfway,
soldiers and statesmen, servants and masters.
The stars stand guard and
form a haze across the vaults
— a few hours when none shall do each other harm.

If we could only speak to each other then
when our hearts are like half-open flowers.
Words like golden bees
would slip through.
— God, teach me the language of sleep.

OLD AGE

I'm more fond of old people.
They sit looking at us and don't see us
and are content on their own,
like fishermen along big rivers,
still as stone
in the summer night.
I'm very fond of fishermen along rivers
and old folks and those who come out after a long
      illness.

They have something in their eyes
that the world doesn't see anymore,
old people, like convalescents
who aren't strong enough on their feet yet,
and with pale foreheads, as after fever.

The old
who gradually become themselves once more
and slowly dissolve
like smoke, unnoticed they pass over
into sleep
and light.

NIGHT MUSIC

The constellations shall change.
The Big Dipper's handle
will stretch south
and Orion shall lose his sword
before the last pain has passed,
says the stone.

Also for me
it is measured out.
Like a fountain's shimmering dust
rises and falls back into itself,
so my days rise from somewhere within me,
measured out in a stone bowl.

There is a calm light over old trees.
They let the wind run through their leaves
and the stars pass high above their crowns
in majestic procession.

THE LIGHT OF MIDSUMMER NIGHT

Midsummer Night is not a real night,
there's an insanity about it, ice around its heart.
due to an anxiety behind the woods
            somewhere,
someone wants to cry out but can't make
            a sound.

The insane flute of the songthrush
thirsts for salvation it cannot have.
The light is filled with someone who wants
            to weep in it,
who has left the plucked flowers behind
            in a field
and now hides his pale face in his hands.

The light of Midsummer Night
shrieks out behind woods and out over
            the lake ice
which now resembles the glowing eyes
            of the madman
who rose higher and higher, dizzily
            through sunlight
and flower-mist. But tonight,
at this hour, he knows for the first time
from his body's desire
his kinship with death.

TOWERS OF SORROW

The slaves had enormous hands and they built
        towers of sorrow.
They had hearts of lead and shoulders like
        mountainsides and they built
        towers of sorrow.
They had hands like sledgehammers and they built
        mountains of silence.

They still stand in Burgundy and Baalbek and Jerez
        de la Frontera.
Ashen walls rising above forests, stone foreheads
        and melancholy eyes,
many places on earth
where swallows weave out in wide sweeps in the air
like silent strokes of a whip.

SUMMER IN THE GRASS

(1956)

SNAIL

Tiny wanderer of grassblades in peace
with trumpet on back and tall horns
like antennae to east and west
for the blind singer, who,
respectful, always
kisses the earth.

Carefully he bends
each blade aside, listens anxiously
for any danger there. Then he plays
on his trumpet the happy
song of the grass.

Homeless, timeless
little friend in the grass who wanders
on a kiss.

MORNING, LET ME PULL YOU CLOSE

Morning, let me pull you close,
all the way into my heart,
all your light, birdsong and deep leaves,
touch you with my hands like a blind man.

With the fingertips of my senses
I touch your face when it comes toward me,
cool as a statue after the night's rain.
But who lives behind those lips,
behind the swift hand that pulls me with it?
And the secret song in your throat . . .
that I will never know.

MOON AND APPLE TREE

When the apple tree blooms
the moon often shows up as a blossom,
paler than any of them,
shining over the tree.

It is the dead summer,
the blossoms' white sister who returns
to see us
and bless us with her hands
so the burden won't be too heavy when hard times
        come.
For the Earth itself is a blossom, she says,
on the star-tree,
pale and with luminous
ocean leaves.

DAWN RAIN

Patient morning rain waits by the gates,
barefoot and in poor dress like a beggar girl

stands in the woods a long time and in the meadows
and waits
wordless by the windows and watches me when I
sleep.

Morning rain, you who walk silently among houses
and gates,
why do you have such peaceful steps and such slow
feet?

Are you the white summer herself. Who has sent you
to people's houses where we no longer notice a poor
dress.

But the fields light up behind you and you give
a vast peace to the grass. Who are you

who wordlessly sings of the loneliness in God's heart
and covers our windows with your blind caress.

OLD PEOPLE'S GRAVES

Old people's graves
are like the graves of adolescents,
very quiet and with sunbleached stones,
but there is more of Earth in them
and deeper solitudes
in the graves of old people.

There's a larger sky in them
and a milder sun since all things
return to themselves.
That's why there should be large trees
with rustling crowns arched
over old people's graves.

A PATH THROUGH GRASS

A path through grass
worn as an old handle
and pale as silver.
The silent things
that build bridges so many places on Earth,
roads after the dead, a handle;
a path through grass
passes like something unreal through summer,
moon-bridges crossing green seas.

IN THE MIRROR, IN THE WATER

This mirror is like a stone,
cool, old and patient;
with wisdom's care
and weariness it shows you
as you are.

See your reflection in the water. It's got the sparkling
eye of youth.
Laughing, it looks at you, erases you
and runs away.

WOMEN'S SLEEP

The sleep of old women is often heavy
and they struggle with so many hard dreams
that bite at their skirts like small children
with strong teeth — all their wounds reopen
and everything is the sweat and haste of long ago
when life gave three or four breaths of courage
and large swollen breasts. Now they want to awaken
but the doors of sleep are too stiff now. They sleep
as deeply as cement and don't know anybody
      anymore.

GOD'S HEART

We don't know God's heart,
but we know
something that pours out over us
like rain over our hands.

We don't see His eyes,
but we see
invisible light over everything
as on a summer night.

We don't hear His voice,
but we find
roads everywhere and signs in our hearts
and paths with hushed light.

GREEN LIGHT

Creatures that rustle in shadow, all the crooked
and deformed in this world, those with tiny feet
        and far too many eyes
can hide in the grass; that's why it's there,
silent and full of moonlight among the continents.

I have lived in the grass with those tiny ones
        who resemble broken twigs.
The bumblebees flew into my heart like bells
        with magical words
from their marigold towers.
The winds took my poem and spread it out like dust.

I have lived in the grass with the Earth, and I have
        heard it breathe
like an animal that has walked far and is thirsty
        for waterholes.
At evening I felt it lie down heavy on its side
        like a buffalo
in the darkness between stars, where there is room.

The wind's dance and the large grass fires come
        back to me often:
shadow images of smiles on a face that always
        shows forgiveness.
But why does it have such patience with us,
deep in the iron core, the huge magnesium heart?
        That we can't understand.

We have forgotten this: The Earth is a star of grass,
a seed-planet, swirling of spores like clouds,
　　　from sea to sea
a driving mist. Seeds bite hold beneath
　　　the cobblestones
and between the letters in my poem. Here they are.

ANTENNAE

The antennae's basting stitch
sews together a new world
with a stitch here and there
between forests and ocean,
but we barely glimpse the pattern,
inverted and reversed.

Thick strong yarn
for humanity's new suit,
cut, but still not worn
with trousers on.

IN COUNTRIES WHERE THE LIGHT
HAS A DIFFERENT COLOR

In countries where the light has a different color
the street faces may be transformed one evening
to pearls in a slow ocean of indigo.

And you have to ask yourself — what is mirrored
by these fire-diadems? What hands
have strewn them on this sea in darkness?

THE DEVIL IN THE TOWER

What do they want?
Words like free oranges
or words with knives between the teeth
like bandits?

Now that the words no longer exist
and the poem has become a rusted mask high
        in a tower,
they have raised toward the swallows
and our Lord.

They want words like robbers,
sentences like footsteps in dark stairs,
and poems with overhead lights as in fancy shops!

But I tell you words no longer exist. And poems
        are like those paintings of the dead
they exhibit in empty churches and castle towers.

Let us make a poem like a devil.
Let's put a dreadful eye in it
and hoist it up on the wind vane
so the swallows can do what they have to on it
and a god can come once in a while and choke
        a smile
and say: Well now.

LETTER TO LIGHT

(1960)

LETTER TO LIGHT

Morning's paper is huge folded out
on the Earth; it is a new day
and a tractor is already out with its lumpy fist
writing a letter to the light; it grumbles
each letter out loud to itself because it matters
        so much
that everything is included, the thunder
        and the bees,
the ant-road that has stretched out its tiny
silken foot in the grass; our peace
and our restlessness about everything has to be
        included.

Large moist lines and a slow hand
that shakes a lot, but now everything is said,
the page is full and everything is exposed
like a letter to no one, the plow's letter
to light that whoever wants to can read.

RIGHT BEHIND YOUR FOOT

Right behind your foot
is the greatest silence
and a wondrous love,
different from anything you know.

Different from all
that you can hear, you can see
— the song after your feet,
the light after your hands.

Right behind your shoulder,
closer than you think, a peace
you have not yet felt,
where the world falls silent
one deep and sudden moment,
as after an unspoken promise
through a closed mouth.

PROFILE OF A BOY

That little world below the knee
has gone to sleep out there; the grass darkens,
but I still see your luminous crescent
low above a branch.
A forehead cut from thin paper,
the growing moon is ringed around your own
but still open, listening to everything
— the grumble of a June bug, the joy-note
          of a thrush,
the snail's moist stripe on a leaf.

And I see you being released from Earth,
a little anxious as you draw your first ice-breaths;
lands sink lower, advancing oceans gleam
and show you an image of yourself: a boat,
          a forehead
harder than my own, a stern profile
that gives you solace and a new kind of peace.
While I have sunk lower than the night.

WRITTEN IN THE WIND

There is something we have forgotten
written in the wind and thunder,
what they have to say.

Rain hammers the windowpanes,
the wind lifts it up and erases it,
the butterfly unfolds its red sail.
We can't remember where we are
— it's on the tip of our tongue
but suddenly it's paralyzed and everything
seems to be behind a veil.

Something we have forgotten,
a leap of time, a language
known before,
everything is silent.

— Something we've forgotten
the letters of rain and thunder we can't read
        anymore,
drawings on snow, everything is lost.
The butterfly suddenly opens its wings
like a flaming mouth and whispers words,
illegible letters
behind stone walls where someone cries
but you cannot help.

MEMORIES OF HORSES

Lines in the hands of old people
slowly curve over and shall soon point toward
        the earth.
That's where they'll take their secret language:
cloud-words and wind-letters,
all the signs the heart gathers in the lean years.

Sorrow is bleached out and turns to face the stars,
but memories of horses, women's feet, and children
flow from their faces over into the grass' kingdom.

In large trees we can often see
images of calm animal flanks,
and the wind draws in the grass, if you're happy,
running children and horses.

SMALL LIGHTS AT SEA

Your hand rests here, an upturned boat
pulled halfway onto the beach,
and full of breathing; like a conch
it waits for you, for your return.

And I can see that someone is still out
at sea, though soon it's completely dark
— fishermen have lit lanterns on their boats
that the waves slowly lift
and lower again, as though searching
with lamps, like fireflies before a huge canvas
so they might make out its incomprehensible
        signature
or bring a face to light,
a color that gives hope.

A TREE

A tree
with all its leaves like open hands,
and the bark's enormous
whale-hide that endures everything.
That lofty silence
where branches spread out like constellations
shining with the same light
and dives down
into the secret land of dark springs.
Cool your hands, rest here
against this breast
where life trickles from its quartz bowl
and doesn't offer you more than you can bear,
and always you're the same — year after year
a tree, the house of birds.

SILENT PICTURE

Into that soiled image of the street,
the truck backing up, in reverse through the gate,
fish wrapping that has lain on the sidewalk
        since spring,
those brown cigarette butts caught
        in the sewer grate,
and the vomit by the house wall
comes an old man with his brown bag
waddling like an old goose, tired of everything.
Infinitely slow he drags his feet forward
through the shadows in front of the open
        garage doors
where clouds of exhaust pour out like ammonia
and turns the corner to the back of this picture
— the stairway with its smell of old grief,
the dark bed, the gas heater and frayed curtains
that slowly hold forth their bowl of light
— vinegar and bile that the stars lift up to us.

GLASS SOLDIERS

Days of hard rain
remind me of soldiers; they have raw hands
and stripes of muddy water in their eyes.

On a thousand feet they pass through the cities
        of Europe
like walls of steel, vertical bayonets,
sharp drums and flutes,
banners faded from lying in the earth so long

— without identity, for they have no faces,
only feet and hands, feet and hands through all
        eternity
past the lukewarm in their doorways: the cowardly
and damned survivors of all wars.

Europe's rain, lukewarm, millenial,
like blood on your face, mud in your eyes,
grape tears, the poppy's red mouth.

LANDSCAPE, PROVENCE

Horizons of slaked lime, chalk-white mountains
that force your eyes slowly down, all light
lashes out like a sword.

Woe on us
that no one can understand
the birds' writing, the cry of mountainsides.
The ocean brings in its marble
and unloads it on the beach.

Old walls are like grey smoke
after wars long since forgotten.
The sky is full of large rivers
that run nowhere
like on canvases by van Gogh.

There are marks after hands in all clouds,
fingers that have touched the light
and become light.

THE SILENCE AFTERWARDS

(1965)

DENSE SNOWFALL

Dense snowfall fills the streets in the morning
like some kind of insanity in the light
— someone who tries to play a flute with amputated
        hands
and cover the traffic lights with lace handkerchiefs—
but it fails and like each effort
to change our world view is itself transformed
to spilled oil and urine and runs down the sewer.

Because it's no use with chloroformed butterflies
or to wipe the sponge slowly over a picture
        that is evil
when the hand hesitates and is unsure of itself
and the picture is of iron.

LIGHT COMES TO THE STONES FIRST

It always comes to the stones first
— light, as though it revolved around blindness.

First to the stones, like a coldness,
rebirth, a cry
without sound.

Night dissolves in fragments,
gradually as each
gravestone reappears,
gutters, rooftops,
but dimly, as if through water
— someone forces his way in to us
and tries to see what no one has seen before,
his forehead meets a wall,
a foot stumbles over rocks.

Maybe your heart, that the night won't give rest.
Your death, but something in your dream
        has to leave first.

THE SIDEWALKS

There are sidewalks for everyting.
There are sidewalks for migraines
and for falling in love under trees.
There are sidewalks where they sell live rabbits
and sidewalks for furs and military bands.
There are sidewalks where they sleep on drainage
        grates,
sidewalks for rush hours and heavy snowfalls.
There are sidewalks for medium-sized worries
and sidewalks for a lost rose.

There are sidewalks that one day shall be present
        at the world's end
and cry out to the heavens and the ocean:
Here we have 'em.

DEADLINE 11 P.M.

Earth's fully automatic rotary press
prints its paper daily for those who can read.
Unaddressed, cataloged in eternity.

Lead figures of the continents are already molded
into tonight's printing blocks. The paper
is silently gathered from the sun spool.
Typesetters slam home the letters of the moment,
like machine gun-fire. Everything shall be included.

Everything. The tears of children, your tie
and the corpse in the suitcase, indigestion,
sinful neglects, your death, even
the color of your stamps.

Lightning flash photographs crucial details.
The nightshift proofreader cuts away
what's directly embarrasing. All the rest is included.

The morning paper is ready. Earth turns.
Now it emerges from the rollers, fragrant
with raw printer's ink, plowed fields,
rivers and marsh mist, gas, oil,
arm sweat and downdraft from the factory
            chimneys.
Everything is included
in the morning paper, printed in one copy
for you, if you want to read.

ABANDONED HOUSES — BYGONE DAYS

Those who walked these paths are dead,
the well is overgrown, and all the houses
sag, asleep like exhausted children.
But the rosebush they planted here in the time
        of hope
still stands heart-red in the middle of its nettle
        garden
and reads its poems for thrush and crow
and burns its light for moss, rust and moth
in the month of June.

THE PRISONER

A park is a summer imprisoned deep in the city,
chained to stone walls so we can all see it.
— Come here, children. This is what summer
      looks like.

And we can throw it crumbs through that iron fence
where the algae-green pond shimmers beneath
      leaves
— this tin plate the wardens have given it.
Maybe a swan glides silently out from the shadow
like the dream of years past, some half-forgotten
      memory.

On the sky's open rectangle it can see
clouds wander past in blissful procession
on their way to its homeland.
The fountain's tired flute
plays low songs of floods.

STRIPTEASE

Hey, there's more.
You're not finished yet.
There's more
Lily
and without wine, Lily
and without men.

For your breasts
and your mouth
must fall
and your pale cheek
Lily
Yeah, come on
Lily
and without glitter
because there is more.

Yeah, without loud music
Lily
and without dance steps, Lily
— your eyebrow
your thin hand
your slender foot must fall
for one who waits
day and night
Lily
behind dark veils.

HEADLINES

(1969)

SSSH

Sssh says the ocean
Sssh says the small wave at the shore — sssh
not so violent, not
so proud, not
so remarkable.
Sssh
says the surf
crowding around the outcrops,
washing the shore. Sssh,
they say to people,
this is *our* Earth,
our eternity.

A POEM IS LIKE A FOREST

— not a whole forest
just a rather small forest
really only a tree
really only the wind in a tree,
but who writes about that
on judgment day?

Today a tree
is something to hide behind
or to hang yourself from
or be shot by.

A tree full of rain like blood
but still a tree
full of snow.

A tree and a tree
and three more trees. A bird
came one day
and filled my tree
with song
then snow came.

Trees, trees
so many thousands they are
— logs, planks, and beams, an army
— le grand armé —
sounding the horn of the southern wind
from Vladivostok around the globe
to Kirkenœr.

Birdsong, winter snow
— moose tracks are what we see
beneath tree after tree

— that we can hang ourselves from
or be shot by.

MOSTLY —

Mostly gravel paths mostly
pebbles and asphalt mostly
flat sidewalks and window reflections
pedestrian crossings car lanes and traffic lights.
Mostly desk lamps and dossiérs single spaced
thin paper and ding from the typewriter.
Mostly glowing cigarettes and hushed words
        in a doorway
and small echoes that fade away with the cars.
Mostly distances behind a face, withheld
words. Indifference
— mostly —

YOUR THOUGHTS, YOUR DEEDS

Your thoughts, your deeds
shall not die,
but your hopes
shall die, your joy,
your needs
shall die, your desires, demands
die but not
what you did,
what you did
despite everything,
did, shamefully
little it is,
but it live,
should have been more,
it lives
but
your desires
shall die, your hopes shall die
soon, but
your thoughts, what were your
thoughts, shall live and
what did you do,
damn, yes, what
did you do
— you.

WHAT WE KNOW

They got us to the moon but most
is unknown, most
is undiscovered.
Cannot be understood, we can't even
imagine

— most
is still wrapped in silence, what we know
is a sparrow, what we know
is a gap in a doorway,
a sudden
raindrop in the eye.

THE WESTERN WIND

The Western wind
    whistles between the ship masts, wants
    to know, wants to speak, wants to change.
The Southern Cross
    is a jewel of fire, a silent symbol.
The rain
    hammers fever-like against the windowpanes
    — don't you understand.
The cowered, the forgotten
    of this world keep to the back streets. They
    keep their words inside them.
    They can't speak.

Those who seek a place to live,
    those who watch their houses burning
    can't speak.
Those the world holds in contempt, the outcasts,
    the smitten can't speak.
The hungry, the thirsty,
    those rummaging through garbage,
    those who collapse in the street, on jungle
    trails, their mouths filled with blood,
    they can't speak.
You can speak.

WATCH THE DOORS —
THE DOORS ARE CLOSING

(1972)

SIGN LANGUAGE.
IMAGES IN SAND

Many languages. Do you
believe what death says. Do you believe in the wind
that runs from house to house

and wants to know everything about us all.
Everything speaks but not everything
arrives. Lips move, fingers
draw images in sand.
Speak us. A word.
Just a little one. As long as
it's a word.

Someone must know the codes
images tapping signals shouts
and echoes of shouts but hurry. Many
are already dead. Most of it
is dust. Gone.

WAIT FOR US

Wait for me says the snail. Why such haste.
I come when I can; remember my feet are still wet.

Far in its forest the cuckoo sings its song.
Wait-wait, hu-hu, wait wait, there's something you
		forgot,
you forgot, forgot.

Wait for me, wait for me, says the snowdrift
		on the mountain.
Let me rest a little longer; I have to melt first.

Hey-hey, wait now, wait wait, shouts the wind.
There's another storm coming, and I have to blow
		down another light tower
up near Valsøyfjord.

Wait for me, mom and dad, cries the child.
I can't see you anymore. I'm scared.

Friends, wait for me, wait up a bit, says old Earth.
I have my timetables to watch. Many lands
that need their daily light.

Wait for us, wait for us, cry the hungry and ragged
		people.
After all, you own the world.
At least light a lamp so we can see where we are.

Hey, you over there. Now wait a bit,
say the kids on the street corner. Where

are our jobs? What are you doing
to our lives? What's the point of it all?
Answer us — before we break another window.

Wait for us, the words plead. Not so fast, not so fast.
This ought to be a poem you'll remember a while.

KNIVES KNIVES

Knives knives everywhere they cut
up the world with knives
without mercy and we must acquiesce
because they want to see the inside of everything
how it's put together
everything your soul and the birdsong
shall be dissected and revealed before the judges
daydreams sex-drive and fear of death
but something has gone wrong for them
they can't put it back together won't grow
remains scattered like butchered meat
wreckage
yellow bones
but the knives keep cutting
every day something is taken away
and the refuse piles grow constantly
— I'm frightened. Soon the sanitary
engineers will call here.

CHANGING LIGHT

Evening and planet
pour their light onto the other side
(out through windows and over hillsides)
so the grey dawn can come to the rice fields
and light may fall on the dead man's breast,
because we are unfeeling
or thoughtless. For us darkness is near
and now the light searches
over fingers lips eyelids
of those who sleep on the street in cities
        of the forsaken
and of the girl with the tired smile
who stands and lets the oxen drink
before thatched huts here
under Mount Djema Oka
which in her language means The Tearless.

Whether it's this way or that
here we have used up our day
and must content ourselves with the Coke ads
        and the moon
and with darkness that extends toward the ends
        of the Earth.

RED AND BLACK

Pitch black tonight.
The tail-light of a car
bursts forth like a drop of blood
runs diagonally down
into the picture
wavers a bit
and is still
until it's swallowed by the darkness
disappears
and everything is
night again.

THE FOG BY ANZIO
(WAR CEMETERY)

Fog-day. Veils fine as spiderwebs
like light flickering from the ocean
over a landscape strangely autumn-frost-white
and ill. Bus stop. Ladies and gentlemen

this is the war's plowland, the stubble-
fields after death.
Veils of ocean mist shall cover it over
but through the half-shadow we see

the reaping machines harvest,
wheat stubs in endless stripes
under the sky where the knives cut
the wheat from Essex, the corn
from the Oregon summer — not a straw
is left standing not a tear not a cry a
living breath only dust
and cement.

Mist-spun seasilk veils flickering before our eyes
will turn it into dreams. Shadowplay.
But soon the wind shall come, sea salt
and tear the veils away. Hard sun shall burn.

MANHATTAN SKYLINE

Glittering horizon. A row of pearl-
white teeth. Will it smile.
Oh baby. No.

Glittering horizon. Razor-sharp spears.
Fangs in a carnivor's jaw,
molars that can crush stars.
Oh baby. Yes.

BREATHING EXERCISE

(1975)

TRAFFIC JAM
(RAINY DAY)

East-west, the windshield wipers say.
That's all you're allowed to see: east-west, west-east.

In a little triangle before your face.
Just stare straight ahead.

East-west, west-east, east-west, west-east
In time like an army. Rank after rank.
Shiny flashes from bayonets.

East-west, west-east, just relax, relax
light a cigarette, lean back in your seat
(east-west, west-east) — and don't sit there feeding
        on illusions.

And remember. Most important (east-west,
        west-east)
don't *SCREAM.*
Because now you're dead stuck.

ASPHALT

First they come with grey gravel
and then they come with black asphalt.
First it's like silk.
Then like steel.

Because everything has to be strong and hard now,
and level of course,
and naked and perfectly smooth
so they can come rolling forth, first on silent rubber.
Then on belts of iron.

First you must learn to keep quiet.
Then you must have the correct opinions.
First it concerns your thoughts.
Then your hopes and dreams.

AUTOBAHN

The asphalt ribbon's black leather whip shrieks
     across a naked land
where sparse forests come marching forth
— fade backward and are gone.

Distances hammer aginst the windshield. A white
     cloud stretches
out its hand and waves
— fades backward and is gone.

Cathedrals and churchtowers — like remnants
of old barbed wire in the distance
— fade backward and are gone.

The roads run into the heavens, but that's delusion.
     Summer
and fall, winter and spring
— fade backward and are gone.

All speed is flight. What are you fleeing? Your hopes,
     your restlessness
— fade backward and are gone.

Night comes suddenly, the world's splendor, you
     yourself
— fade backward and are gone.

ANTENNA FOREST

On the cities' roofs are vast plains.
That's where the silence crawled when there wasn't
      any room for it on the streets.
Now the forest follows.
It has to be where the silence is.
Tree follows tree in strange clusters.
But it doesn't get it quite right because the floor
      is too hard.
It makes a sparse forest, one branch to the east,
one to the west. Until it resembles a cross. A forest
of crosses. And the wind comes and asks
— Who sleeps here
in these deep graves?

SKY-HIGH HOUSES

The sky-high houses stand and wonder if they are
        gods.
Up in their clouds they stand and look down
        on the people.
We are like the sun, they think. We are like the stars.
Deathless. With faces of snow and ice.

Down in the depths it darkens from the multitudes
        that never calm down.
Bundles of light are thrown to them like bread,
        with the crack of dogwhips.
For they are unbearable. — What good is it all, they
        cry.
Give us a faith, a meaning in it all.

The high houses stand and look at each other
        with crystal eyes.
What shall we do with the people, they wonder.
We give them toys to shut them up. We let them
        get drunk
so they can forget. And they still don't know
        what they want.
Shall we bring them the sun?
Or snuff out the stars?

PROBLEM II

. . .whatever we do
the machines
only move the hunger two stairs up;
now it sits in the heart.

BREATHING EXERCISE

If you go far enough out
you can only see the sun as a spark
in a dying fire
if you go far enough out.

If you go far enough out
you can see the entire wheel of the Milky Way
roll away on roads of night
if you go far enough out.

If you go far enough out
you can see the Universe itself,
all the billion light years summed up time
only as a flash, just as lonely, as distant
as a star on a June night
if you go far enough out.

And still, my friend, if you go far enough out
you are only at the beginning

— of yourself.

TO EARTH (with friendly greetings)

Listen Earth, we have something to tell you
— not because we don't like it here, this is a fine
       place,
plenty of water and high and airy under the roof,
we lay seeds in the earth and soon the gold sways
       in the fields,
you have given us almost everything,
oil and rich oceans and wool for winter,
but we have no peace here anymore.
Something has jarred us off course;
we walk around in fear
of all that can happen.
That's why we ask you now: What do you do
       with your mountainsides and oceans?
How do you manage to keep your inner balance,
always in equilibrium. You follow your path in space
faultlessly, not straying an inch,
soundless, alone behind all the light years
       in eternity,
with only a slow roar from the ocean
and from the wind through the forests now
       and then.
You put on a new sun and wind and spring comes
       as expected.
All the arithmetic dissolves, your figures
       and patterns
are clear as crystals.
That's why we come to you and ask
how you manage it.

For we have lived with you so long, in desire
        and need,
and from you we have gotten what we needed,
except that one thing — equilibrium and constancy,
your undisturbable calm.
Yes, you see yourself what has happened to us,
how we transform life to death wherever we go
— the factories that work day and night
        on extermination weapons
while millions of us live like animals, in hunger
        and need.
In East and West the slums grow like a disease
and have already formed a crust around the large
        cities,
you see it yourself, and, well, we can't stop it
— not without torrents of slaughter, bloody
        holocausts.

You who guide the icebergs into milder seas
and let summer silently turn into autumn, each
        to its time,
and let spring burst forth as green fountains
        after the snow
— lend us some of your balance, your calm,
as when night turns into day and the bad weather
        disappears over the hills,
you must help us rebuild our house
that will soon collapse and crush everybody.

We're sure you will miss us. It would be very quiet
        here.
Strange and silent when the fields grow over

and all the oceans are deserted.
— And what will you say at night, to all the stars
when they come and crowd around you
with cool professor-eyes gleaming
behind their stern eyeglasses:
—well now, what happened to our incubator.
Did the experiment fail?

LOOK —

The moon thumbs through night's book.
Finds a lake where nothing is printed.
Draws a straight line. That's all
it can.
That's enough.
Thick line. Straight toward you.
— Look.

THE ROCKING BOULDER

That old boulder on the north side of the ridge
lies like a gland within eternity,
burdened by time.
It sucks up the iron light from all the stars.
The winds of the ages brush it slowly across
       the forehead.
Everything is alive. That rocking stone. It knows
       the moon
and the snake that comes when it's sunny.
The last million years have passed quickly.
The rocking stone. Soon it's as old as God.

WEEVILS AND DADDY LONG-LEGS

Many strange things under rocks.
Creatures that resemble paper cuttings,
knitted socks, bits
of wire or yarn.

That God sat and made while waiting here,
to make the centuries pass
—trouser buttons, string
and crumbs of old bread.

But he got the birds right. Their song.
Fluttering wings
that make hearts beat.

Now he sits and spins nebulae
that look like snails,
jellyfish and remnants of old yarn.

THE FJORDS IN AUGUST

Late in August when it calms down
the ocean comes in to rest a while
by Bringa and Beiteln and Brattabroti, tired of being
      ocean
all the time and storms and crashing waves
      all the time.
It carefully opens gate after gate
to hall after hall
and finds a beach at last,
a granite scree, a singing waterfall
and lies down to wonder
about all the things it never got to see
and never understood. The ocean
that comes from storms and knows what death is
and what eternal unease is
finds a little pebble on a beach
stretches out a finger and rolls it around
again and again. Mirror
relieves mirror. Day
relieves night. Mountainsides,
slopes and trees heavy
with fruit.
Forehead against forehead. Arm against arm.
Late August. Green, sometimes golden. And red
as a sleeping cheek.

ENOUGH TIME

Enough time.
The man with the white cane has enough time.
    He's blind.
He knows the world from the inside. The studs
in the wall and snowflakes in hair when autumn
    comes.
He knows what dreams are made of.

He belongs to the day, not the night.
He can tell from your voice if your heart is at peace.
The light lays a finger on his mouth.
Don't ask him. He knows more than you.

There is a world beyond the eyes.
Larger than ours. It is his.
If he takes your hand he feels its bones
like birdwings.

YOU HAVE IT IN YOU

You have it in you.
Far inside you someplace.
The yellow, staring eye. And the thought
that is colder than ice.

Inside you and well-hidden:
The staring eye that can pierce walls.
And the thought (God help us all)
sharper than a sword.

What are we doing?
Giving it over to the night?
Well-hidden.
Yes.
No.

WITHOUT A SOUND

The silence within all that happens.
The weight of the unspoken. The light
that falls on a face
as change, not as peace.

Someone stands there, unaware of existing.
Sounds fall to the earth. Rain
shatters like glass.

The unfathomable has no voice.
The important things. Not night darkness.
Not sunlight. Not death.

WINTER POEM

Winter again.
And dark.
The sun sticks in a red eraser.
Look here, rub it all out.
Everything.
Write it again.
White paper — use the whole sheet.
Now we want your answer.

IT WAS TODAY

We don't understand this. That it was today
he died. That it was today
they nailed his hands to the wood.

That it was today
he stiffened in death. That they loosened the nails
and carried him into the tomb.

Light as a bird and cold as snow.
That it is today
he is no more.

PLOWS

Time for plows.
They rip up, cut away
and lay everything carefully down.
Year after year upside-down, upside down
            —everything

so dark earth comes forth
naked, fresh, and moist.
Turn it around, flip it.
What has been in darkness shall have light.

Cut carefully. This knife resembles a boat.
Its wake straight as a line.
Age after age.
Plow furrows. Waves against a shore.

THINK ABOUT SOMETHING ELSE

(1979)

TURN AWAY — THINK ABOUT SOMETHING ELSE!

— Turn away. Think about something else.
Think about everything you can buy. Think about
       your car.
Everything in the advertisements. Elegant things.
Don't stand there looking this way the whole time.
       Turn.
Think about something else, we've said.

Well, turn then! Look in the shop windows.
Tremendous things. The latest in all the lines.
Sealskin coats. Isn't that something? New suit.
It's spring soon. Think of gorgeous girls.
Think about hoo-whee! Well, but turn then.
We haven't asked for witnesses here.
Go to a movie tonight or to church
if you're that kind. Join in the hymn-song,
be like the others, damn it!

Listen now. For the last time. Don't look this way.
Think about something else. We've told you now
— we don't want an audience here.
Buy yourself a thick newspaper or a magazine.
Look at all the color pictures, and remember this is
       the last warning.
— That's it. That's fine. And now we'll talk about
       something else.

No, damn it! Stay there.
Or we shoot.

THE NEW DEATH

The new death
is different from the old one.
It moves more quietly on stairs,
almost on stocking feet,
and comes more often to the young
in dirty attic rooms
or dark cellars.
— No matter what they say:
They die of hunger
(and a new kind of hunger).
Because too many are full
(of a new kind of fullness).

TO GROW DOWNWARD

The bigger the cities grow
the smaller the people become.
The higher the houses thrust toward the clouds
the lower those who must live there become.
In New York you are only 10 centimeters.
In London and Singapore maybe an English foot.
And the cities grow and grow
and your life gets to be worth less and less.
Soon we are only as tall as grass-tufts,
to be cut with a lawnmower
early one Sunday morning.
Or what do you think?

THE CORRIDORS

The world organism's
new arteries:
— the corridors,
the road network for those waiting
with or without hope.
Always on foot,
same distance
back and forth.
Your solace:
One time
you'll be relieved of the return.

THE CHURCH ON WALL STREET

On Wall Street I found an old church
half squeezed to death between skyscrapers of glass
        and marble.
The white money towers pointed solemnly toward
        the sky,
but the old church stood there humbly
        with an outstretched hand
and rang its little bell, so someone might hear
        and see.

                *   *   *

Prisoner-for-life or hostage. At least they let it live
down in the shadow there. Maybe some would come
— so it made itself a little useful. Because this they
        know, the mighty,
that it pays, it pays
to give a flower to the poor once in a while
and a dime to an old servant
in the house of the rich.

IN ALL FORESTS THERE HAVE LIVED PEOPLE

In all forests there have lived people.
They stared at the forest edge. And the years
        went by them.
They stared at the clouds. But so little helped.

That's why all our forests
are so sparse at the edge, notched
like sawblades, or ragged borders,
frayed fringes.
They are worn down from all those waiting eyes
and yearnful glances
that looked and looked and looked
to see if anyone came.

And some came.
But usually too late.
Most didn't come.
Only winter came, and autumn rain
and the white face beneath the coughing fits
came. But most of all it was quiet,
and once in a while they carried a coffin away.

                *   *   *

It's great to walk in the forest, and best in large
        ones.
And hear the rustling through the trees
and what it murmurs about with dark voices.

Mumble-mumble, says the forest.
So far away, so far away.

But more you never get to know,
never, never, never get to know.

And soon now
all the houses in the forest
are empty.

OTHER TRAINS

Every day poverty's trains leave for the cities
in endless caravans, bundles, ox carts,
from hunger's land to the street's lonesomeness
— near the houses of the rich where they think there
        is hope.

Every day other trains leave the cities
        for the country,
not too long yet, but they grow, they grow.
They break away from the death, the loneliness,
        shame,
for an unknown land. If our dreams were shattered
hope still lives. Otherwise we'd be dead.

STRANGE

Full moon out. The first snow has come.
An old tree stands and lifts its arms.
Stands calling.
Strange with a white land at night
— almost silver.
And strange with so large a moon
— almost golden.
And the old tree that lifts its arms to shout:
— Release us
from ourselves!

SITUATION (FROST NIGHT)

All the cigarette butts froze to the sidewalks
and the matchsticks to the gutters
all the way down Hegdehaug Street.
— First night of frost, they said on the radio.
Even the words froze in the air.
Everything they said to each other
— some here and some there —
melted only when they got back inside,
some maybe as a tiny wet spot
in the corner of your eye.
Some as a warmth in you. Red in your cheeks.
Or some remained, perhaps
as a frost
the winter through.

MORNING SOUND. AUGUST

Rain tonight.
All sounds
large as houses.
Trees stand full of song.
The streets lie wet. Pale sun
strains behind the curtain. The swallows' songs
already announce
that summer is going away. Slowly
our little city begins to awaken.
The newspapers are late today. Everything is late.
And now it starts raining again, hair-like strands
dense against the windowpane. Silver dust, a silk
      veil
around everything green.
Light-shimmer.
Where are *you* when I am gone?

FOG DAY. SOLACE

Another foggy day, mild. A little frost
on each tree. Someone
applies gauze
and soft compresses.
Thin strips of cotton
gently, carefully between each tree,
each bush,
between each house. Should we move now?
Has something happened to us?

Ah,
a sun
so distant, so remote
presses slowly forward like clotting blood
behind the bandages. Bleeding
that hasn't quite been stopped.
But the fog takes it. The fog wipes away everything.
All the fall fragrances of phenol and ether
are dampened by white sheets of snow,
so clean they sparkle.

So, stay calm. Everything will be just fine,
just fine, just fine, just fine.
In spring we'll go out and walk again.

IF YOU'RE WILLING

Do you have enough
warmth?
You do.
Sleep, thoughts
are given you freely.
But the warmth inside you
you must give
and give again.

You too
can speak a word of joy.
You have a hand,
warm
if you're willing.

NOW

Now is
when you read this
before you forget again.
Now
this piece of etenity,
a microsecond
slips through your hands, through your eyes
like a snowflake, trickling pearl,
arrow cutting through air
before it strikes.

The cutting edge of all that's been
and has never happened before.

Now
you're older already
since that first line. Now
is like water falling,
a beating heart. Now
a cloud passes before the sun. Now
the birds flew away. And now
you've already forgotten.
Turn the page
or move on.

"JAWS"

Black holes
that swallow stars,
chew solar systems
and spit them out again,
that's the latest news
from the wise men.

Black holes
like the jaws of sharks
thoughout the Universe.
If we're swallowed thus
there is neither time
nor existence,
say those who know.

Only a death
deeper than death
and a birth
no one knows of.

But poor Jonah,
they spat him out again,
but that was just a whale and they're kinder.
— Wonder what they'll know of this
in a thousand years?
Or what they'll think of us
in just a hundred?

THE LITTLE FARMER

It's the little farmer
that is the loser in this world.

It's the little farmer
that has fallen in all the wars,

the little farmer, wherever he lived,
that they took the earth from and whose farm
        they burned

on the way to all their wars. His sons they took
and clothed them in clown suits and let them die

for thoughts he didn't know, nor cared about
and didn't want to know.

It's the little farmer that has to move from his valley
to the assembly lines and factory halls.

It was the little farmer they took the cows from
and the fields for the new highway.

It's he who lies awake at night to pay off his loans
so they can build huge houses that resemble castles.

It's him they have hounded into the cities
and filled the apartment houses with.
        (He'll adapt, all right.)

It's the little farmer who has milked the cows
and removed the rocks from all the fields
where we now can leisurely sow and harvest.

It's the little farmer who knew how the barley
        was sown
and how the calves came to be.

He knows the clouds and the wind, and winter
—if it'll be harsh. He knew well

the neighing of horses. Now he knows the tractor
and the interest on his loan, when it must be paid.

But he still has his door open a crack, the little
        farmer.
He hears when the grass grows
and when the earth gives life again.

He who has lost. For now.
But maybe we must ask him soon

about the way. Where we came from.
Where it grows.

THE PLOWS

Rosewood is the name of this place,
next stop Olathe, then Kansas City.
Ten minutes for a hamburger and a Coke.
Not many houses, just endless tractors.
Plows, plows beneath a diesel mist.

I stand under an old tree
they have spared.
It rumples my hair and asks:
Stranger, what do you want here?

Well, I want to stare at the plows.
They advance like an army across the fields.
Bird flocks follow in the air like a fog.
Dive after earthworms, swup swup,
all the tiny drops of blood
that are found where the Earth still lives.

Plows are like shovels. They bury what is old.
They are like swords. The new shall come up
            into the light.
What was life yesterday, lies today with head down
and legs in the air. What was night and despair
            yesterday
now lies in the light, slowly draws its breath
and comes to life. And now we see
what follows. Soon
it's green here
and then gold — as in the banks. And then

the plows return with their swords
and their shovels. And the birds return
to claim their red drop
of blood.
Yours, maybe?

ROSES — ROSES

— Morning comes with roses.
Rain or sun, always with roses,
still wet with dew. A whole lap full.
One for you. One for me. One for your love.
Here — take it.
A rose.

For all the living.
In through the window. Before your foot.
A rose

for the man who is to be shot at dawn
and sits and listens for the footsteps in the corridor
and the clinking of the keys. Here — take it.
A rose.

A rose for the woman opening the window
on the 28th floor. Take it. A rose to the prisoners
who hear the cries from the next cell.
                    And for the man
whose hands tremble so.
Help him then — Here:
A rose.

Roses — roses
for the blind one. To he who never, never
can get up again. A rose for the junkie in the attic.
She who can hardly see it. And all those thousands
who stand and stare behind barbed wire.
One for each.

Yes.

Morning after morning wet with dew.
Some reach for them in the air. Tired.
Many let them lie. Wither
until only the stalk is left.

The one with thorns. The sharp ones.
Those that can make bloody furrows on foreheads
and a narrow red line
above the temple and down
the left cheek.

BLACK MAN

It was our youngest brother who came
out of those dark forests.
He inherited the Earth's face, the soil's.
And he still had a breast full of song
and big smiles. That no one answered.
Our youngest brother.

We refused to know him.
But he got to know us,
his brothers, in our struggle for power and glory.
And he was strong. As if carved from black oak
and had song in him, the forest's,
and laughter from white teeth.

Our new brother
who had the Earth's face,
and got to suckle the Earth's breast longest.
Maybe it will be he — in the end,
who inherits everything.

NIGHT OPEN

(1985)

TWILIGHTS

Don't believe in the day.
  Night is a little death.
    The twilight is where our life is.

Our thoughts fly high as swallows then.
  Colors glow. And birds are happiest.
    Evenings are grand when you're young.

Dawn is the joy of old people.
  Earth, this paradise star, lets the day begin
    East of East near the Fiji islands.

First the snows of Mount Fuji sparkle.
  Then Mount Everest and last
    blue Aconcagua.

Valleys and plains join in last.
  In the evening it's reversed.
    Mountains must wait.

Dawn and dusk. In twilight zones you must be
  aware. The outline of a face.
    The cheekbones of your life.
      You see more clearly then.

Moments for wonder. Hours when things take form.
  Day comes with a rose in its hand.
    Night with a streak of blood.

TRUTH

Truth waits outside your door.
Dressed in rags. She is ill.
She has a child on her arm. She wants in.
Do you hear the dogs barking? She is afraid.
What do you do? If you open
it will change your life.

Do you hesitate?
You, too.

NEVER BEFORE

Never before
have we had such deep chairs
and wide sofas around our butts.

Never before
have the technocrats made such wonders
        of the world
that our hearts become so anxious
that we have to go into hiding behind ourselves.

Never before
did words need to be shouted so loudly,
and images and sound taken in with cola
to draw our thoughts away and make us harmless.

Never before so urgent. Never before
have we longed so
for a human voice behind the words,
truth and the warmth of a heart behind
        the crows' cry.

CORAL

From their anchor on the deep sea floor
in the death kingdom of the lantern fish
they grow upward unnoticed,
generation upon generation,
layer upon layer
through a thousand years, maybe ten thousand,
until sudden as a shout of triumph
thundering light bursts in.
Now they see the sun.
Small waves light as kisses,
white arms embracing.
Soil comes, rain comes,
sprouting seeds come flowers
come palm up, up
toward the crown of light.

NORTH

Look North more often.
Go against the wind, you'll get ruddy cheeks.
Find the rough path. Keep to it.
It's shorter.
North is best.
Winter's flaming sky, summer-
night's sun miracle.
Go against the wind. Climb mountains.
Look north.
More often.
This land is long.
Most is north.

JAM — JAM

Loud noise.
Breakdance, drums and trumpets
push anxiety away. Make noise.
Jet-start, juke-boxes, jam-jam
for peace and freedom. Fully
freaked out.
But only outside, not within.
It lasts only briefly,
not even through the night.
So do it again. Make noise.
Decibels. Heavy metal. Don't think.
Howl,
louder,
more.

ASK AGAIN

The row of numbers laughs at us
and wants to explain everything.
It has jaws of iron and clattering
teeth.

We ask and ask
and the numbers answer,
but not of violins
or the joy of being embraced.
The screen will cough
—unclear question.
Ask again.

CALM DOWN

They ask and they ask. Why in the world
do we sit here working with letters,
rhythms and punctuation when they want tunes,
moving images. Push a button. Words
that only hum in your ears.
Letters
have to be like boxing gloves. Bang
— right in your face so you stagger.
Otherwise it's no use.

The age of tiredness.
We must realize this soon.
Stress, career, the anxiety and pain
of having no future.
— Thanks, but we've got enough
of our own problems.

Yes, that's fine.
But the question is: How tired are you,
really? How far have you gone
with your life? Why do you lie awake
at night? We understand you
but don't give up.

Because the word is like the grass.
It's just there. Cut it down,
make a lawn that you can trample.

Go ahead, trample it.
It shoots up
unstoppable as long as there is earth. Soon,
before you know it, it's up
between your fingers.
— So calm down.

LISTEN, LITTLE ONE

Listen, little one. The new priesthood
also has its Latin and "Our Father."
Now you have new litanies to learn,
new prayers which no one understands,
— not even now.
And we must keep still. Technocrats
who traded liturgical robes for white coats
and built their churches in all countries
topped with strange domes, and slender towers
that look strangely like crematorium chimneys
— they request we ask no more.
But just have faith. One more time,
little one, you
who stand watching through the iron fence,
what they're doing.

                    *   *   *

They speak, little one, of secret powers
from the depths of the Universe. The actual source
        of life.
And if they succeed we'll all be gods
and all will become gold — become gold.
So don't bother us, they say,
with your questions (We also fear
the outcome.) but kneel
down humbly. There is no hope
other than here
in our hands,
in our houses (Some say they resemble
crematoriums).

*   *   *

But old Earth turns around
and round and yawns
a bird to sleep and the moon up from the ocean.
So tired of her children who are noisy
all the time. Here I lie,
she thinks, with open lap.

With heavy seas, high and low tides, sun
and tremendous storms.
But no one BELIEVES me. Am I already too old?
They don't seem to dare.
They're playing with fire, now. Like the children
        they are.
Soon the house will burn down. What will
        they do then,
said the Earth, before it passed over
into sleep, and all the birds
went silent.

(Written for the 1980 Swedish referendum on nuclear power.)

GRASS,

as invincible as hope.
If you don't watch it
it's up between your fingers,
along the sidewalks or between the feet
of the national monument.
After just a year
you can see a tinge of green over the battlefields
or catch a fragrant trace
across the ashes of a bombed city.
Unquenchable as life itself
or forgetfulness.

Poor people's solace. (The rich
have lawn mowers.) But the grass
minds no one
or everyone. Earth's gift
is stronger than Eros. Endures everything.

Try walking barefoot one morning in June.
Feel how it bends beneath your foot
and straightens again. Washes your feet
like Christ did the disciples'.
Full of goodness, but silent. Even
the man holding the sickle is merely a breath,
        a laughter.

Because grass is everywhere. It grows
and comes back like life itself
or days past. And this I'm leaving
but not fully.

SUDDENLY. IN DECEMBER

Suddenly. In December, I stand to my knees in snow.
Speak to you and receive no answer. You're silent.
Love, so it has happened. Our whole life,
the smile, the tears and the courage. Your
         sewing machine
and all the waking nights. Our travels at last:
   — under the snow. Under the brown wreath.

Everything went so fast. Two staring eyes. Words
I didn't understand that you repeated
         and repeated.
And suddenly nothing more. You slept.
And now they lie here, all the days, the summer
         nights,
the grapes of Valladolid, the sunsets in Nemi
   — under the snow. Under the brown wreath.

Swiftly as though a switch was flipped,
all traces of images behind the eye are dimmed,
erased from the slate of life. Or aren't they?
Your new dress, my face and our stairs
and all that you carried to the house. Is it gone
   — under the snow? Under the brown wreath?

Dearest friend, where is our joy now,
the good hands, the young smile,
your hair glowing above your forehead,
         your courage
and this abundance of life and hope?
   — Under the snow. Under the brown wreath.

Friend beyond death. Take me down to you.
Side by side. Let us see the unknown.
Here is so empty now and this age darkens.
Words are so few and no one hears anymore.
Dearest, you who sleep. Eurydice.
    — Under the snow. Under the brown wreath.

AN INTERVIEW
WITH ROLF JACOBSEN

OLAV GRINDE: Rolf, perhaps you can say a little about the experiences — and what happened in your mind and heart — that led to your first book, *Earth and Iron.*

ROLF JACOBSEN: It took a while before I understood that the pen was my tool. I tried the brush and the drawing pencil. But I understood after a while that it was the pen that could express my thoughts, desires, images, and hopes. Already in high school I was preoccupied with Icelandic sagas and the language form I found there. The Elder Edda and the old skaldic poetry. Free verse without structured meter — rhythm, but without meter. I wondered for a long time if this couldn't also be a new poetic form for our time. I got hold of Carl Sandburg and a Dane by the name of Johannes V. Jensen who used this type of form. It gave me the courage to try. I soon realized that some of the things I wrote were worthwhile. I sent in a collection of my poems to a publisher. And in 1933, *Earth and Iron* came out. I received very fine criticism; it was as if everyone was waiting for a renewal in our poetry. We had lived so long in the shadow of Henrik Ibsen and Bjørnstjerne Bjørnson. The national liberation of 1905 had mobilized half-nationalistic and romantic forces. We received the beginnings of a new social literature, but everyone was wishing a fuller literary renewal. Before the '40s a number of others began writing in open verse. You really only had to open the door to Europe — that's how they were writing everywhere.

O.G.: You mention a freedom and clarity that you found in the oldest extant Norse literature. Did you feel that your day's literature was lacking something essential?

R.J.: Yes. I found that this verse with rhyme and rhythm, with its strict language form, really couldn't cover the new reality. And we really had a new reality — which no one had written poetry about. We had cinemas and railroads, sewers and airplanes and all that, and you just couldn't make poetry of it with the old metrical forms. So it all started in France in the middle of the last century, this "vers libre." There's a poet who said poets threw out rhyme at the same time that women threw away their corsets. With this free verse one could, to a much larger degree, pull the new world, the new reality, into poetry.

O.G.: In your first book I feel the emphasis is placed on "earth" rather than "iron."

R.J.: Yes, I have to explain that. My environment had switched between city and country. I was born in Oslo, but when I was six we moved to the countryside. I went through a second birth. There were no longer cement sidewalks and cement doorways. I escaped all that. I came out into a new living reality. I am sure that my relationship with nature owes much to these formative experiences. Then I went back to Oslo to study at high school. So I've always had one leg in the green and one in the grey, one in nature and one in technological reality. I found my own niche in the technological where no poet had been before. At least not in our country.

O.G.: After your second book, in 1935, there was a long pause, sixteen years, before your third book appeared. Why?

R.J.: Yes, there was a pause. A pause caused in part by well-known world events. I was half-finished with a collection when the war broke out. But after the war I didn't go along with the fad of writing heroic poetry. I had to find myself again. Rediscover a world turned totally upside down. Associate with a new reality and make it a part of my own. Such things take time if one is going to be honest and thorough. So I took the time I needed, until 1951, when I published *Express Train*.

O.G.: Is it possible for a poet in Norway to make a living as a writer?

R.J.: There are a few who can, but they have to write tremendously. We do have one of the world's best grant programs, with much of the money going to writers. We are allocated 200-300 grants, whereas we should have 600. And that's for authors, actors, ballet dancers, painters, and composers — though the writers form the majority of the recipients. The state then guarantees you a certain income, and if your books earn less, they pay you the difference. But the guarantee is much too low. And then we have 50-60 of these three-year grants of almost $9,000 per year. I've received that for a number of years. But then one year I had good income from my books. Together with my small pension, it's not bad. And another year I received a travel grant for about $4,000. So we took an America-trip. The grant system is really pretty good. Then of course the government buys a thousand copies of each book of literature for its libraries. And the acceptance rate is about 90%.

O.G.: In America today so many poets and professors and others still feel that the English poetry and literature of this century is central, and in fact its epitome.

R.J.: We don't have that impression in Norway. American literature had its flowering in the Hemingway years, and English literature perhaps with Eliot and Pound — who really were American. French has had its influence, German, Bertolt Brecht, Spanish, Italian. Many Latin American writers are becoming better known. We'll be hearing more from Latin America. In Europe our attention has been drawn toward Greek and Turkish Poetry. And Africa's voice is gaining strength. I welcome all literatures translated into Norwegian; but we have too few translators. We have to realize we face an internationalization of literature in the years ahead. Our world is too cramped today. I think we need to realize that the world is larger than the North

Atlantic. I don't feel English has dominated this century. Of course English is taught in the Norwegian schools. And if you watch television it comes in handy. Perhaps in business and commerce the English language dominates. But not in literature.

O.G.: Perhaps the translator's role today is to share with us the seeds that have been opened by artists of other languages. And through translation allow these seeds to find new fertile soil.

R.J.: Yes.

O.G.: In his autobiography, *I Confess I Have Lived,* Pablo Neruda, the Chilean Nobel-prize poet, writes about reading before audiences of tens-of-thousands. But in the United States and in Europe a couple of hundred people is considered a very fine turnout for a poetry reading. I wonder why that's so.

R.J.: Probably where Neruda read poetry for tens-of-thousands they didn't have television and mass-media as developed as here. I think that's one of the reasons; but there are others. We've developed an entertainment industry dominated by commercialism. Powerful forces in all countries try to earn money by pleasing the public. Poetry now has a competitor it can't defeat. I think we have to realize that the time of the great poets, those with great big hats and bow ties, poets as prophets, is long past. It was over before World War II. Today we're dealing with a different public.

Of course all poets want to be read. I for my part try to make my poems as clear and understandable as possible, but still realize that poetry has relatively few readers.

O.G.: But is it an elite?

R.J.: No, I wouldn't say that. Some insist that there's elite culture for the educated and a mass culture for the masses. Maybe there's something to that, but I can't fully accept it. When I've been asked who I write for, I say I write for the half-tired. This is an age of tiredness. We don't like ourselves in the society of today, this world we have now. We become tired too quickly. We stress ourselves. Most of us don't have time to acquaint ourselves with the problems of the day. They throw themselves in an armchair and switch on the television. Those are the dead-tired, and they exist in all social classes. I write for the half-tired, those who still possess some curiosity, and still have the ability to wonder, wrestle with a question. Take a book in hand and read it before bed at least. Those are the ones I write for. I think books of poetry, at least in our country, are received by a small but good audience embracing all social classes. I believe this division into elite and mass culture is problematic. It doesn't agree with reality. I believe the secret of a poem lies in its form. A poem is an extension of language. A poem is not a poem if you can say it better with prose. So the poem is an extension of prose. If you can't express it with prose, you have to reach toward poetry, have to reach for the paintbrush, for music, for the abstract symbolism of mathematics — that is all an extension of the human tongue, our means of contact; and poetry is a part of that. We seek to stretch language past its boundaries into the unknown, to cover things, re-write, conquer things that can't be said with ordi-nary language. The spoken and written language has its limitations. We have so many cliches today. It costs a lot to strip them away, to find a language. If one has written a poem and has found an utterly precise and expressive expression, one feels the same as a botanist who has found a new flower, or an astronomer who's discovered a new star — we've conquered part of the Universe. One has expressed what no one has been able to express before. That's precisely where the balance lies between popularity and difficulty; the difficulty is to rework the form so as to make visible what has been invisible.

O.G.: But perhaps the poet often expresses what the reader has already felt and thought, and in this way helps the reader to find his own clearer human-ness, his own place in the world?

R.J.: Yes. I think so. I think we can help those who can handle the poem. Those who read a poem can often feel a sense of liberation — here it is! Here is what I meant. We need many kinds of poets. Poetry shouldn't be homogenized. I have called my kind of poet "observers." Our task is to notice things others don't notice. Our task is to be watchdogs who warn of danger or of things going the wrong way. But I am not one of those who feels the poet should come with solutions to our problems. I stick to old Ibsen's words, "I only pose the question; my task is not to answer." I find no solution. But I point to problems that people haven't noticed yet. Hey, this you've overlooked! Haven't thought of. But if we're aware of it, we can also find the solution. The challenge of poetry is to contribute to change in the inner life, and that may in turn give rise to changes in our outer lives.

O.G.: I notice that in your recent books you point more and more to dangers. But it's not a hopeless doomsday pointing. You give me the feeling that there is hope, but we must hurry and change the direction we, the whole world, are headed.

R.J.: Yes. I can't put it better myself. I think it is urgent. We all feel anxiety about tomorrow and see no light, no solution to it all. But I am old. I have lived through two world wars. Maybe it's my optimism. I have always had doomsday just around the corner all my life. And somehow it has always passed. Never as good as we hoped; never as bad as we feared. I have no patent solution. I only come with an appeal to preserve the Earth. I try to get people to understand that the Earth is a mechanism, an ecological whole. Everything depends upon everything else. We can't keep cutting down the forests, covering it all with asphalt and polluting. I wrote that over thirty years ago: "Industrial District" in 1933, "Oil Catastrophe" in 1956, "Asphalt" in 1975. Now the politicians realize it and come running to pluck votes. I mean the poet has to walk ahead, bark, and signal danger.

O.G.: You mention the world as a mechanism. But from your poems I feel you see the Earth itself, the whole, as a living being.

R.J.: Yes. I can't explain it other than to say that I feel something somehow connects everything, connects human beings to a Whole we haven't discovered yet. I think we've only discovered parts of reality. Most is still unknown. Maybe those living fifty years from now will look back and laugh at us, our beliefs and illusions, our self-confidence that we knew it all.

You will find more of Rolf Jacobsen's poems in
The Silence Afterwards: Selected Poems of Rolf Jacobsen
translated by Roger Greenwald,
Princeton University Press,
and in
Rolf Jacobsen: Twenty Poems
translated by Robert Bly,
The Seventies Press.